ALL OUR FRIENDS

Simple Rewards
of
Simple Living

D.S. Hartley

www.trafford.com

North America & international
toll-free: 1 888 232 4444 (USA & Canada)
phone: 250 383 6864 ♦ fax: 250 383 6804
email: info@trafford.com

The United Kingdom & Europe
phone: +44 (0)1865 722 113 ♦ local rate: 0845 230 9601
facsimile: +44 (0)1865 722 868 ♦ email: info.uk@trafford.com

10 9 8 7 6 5 4 3

ALL OUR FRIENDS

Simple Rewards
of
Simple Living

D. S. Hartley

The original version of *All Our Friends* was serialized
in part in the *Island Tides* newspaper.

for
Erich

Death falls, as at times it must, and Life springs in its place. Nature lives and journeys on and passes all about in well balanced, orderly array.

– Grey Owl

Contents

Chapter 1
The Faery Garden

Call it a dream. Or you can call it a mid-life crisis. You could even call it temporary insanity. You'd probably be closest to the truth if you called what led us to give up fourteen years of the good life in Germany and move back to British Columbia's Southern Gulf Islands in the summer of 1995 all three of the above.

This was not the first time that either my husband or I had left security and routine at the crossroads, and turned off onto a less trodden path. Although we had grown up on different continents, we had both moved often from childhood on. Our lack of firm roots had made us mobile, adaptable and restless at times, and the personal and professional decisions we had made long before we met strayed from the conventional career-family-house pattern. Because new experiences were more valuable to us than material possessions or social status, we never dreaded change like a bank of storm clouds on the horizon, but welcomed it like a rainbow across the sky.

My husband and I started our life together in 1980 in a converted step van that we bought in Saskatoon, Saskatchewan, and drove out to the West Coast. For the next year and a half we lived in our Dede on Salt Spring and Pender Islands, and travelled to California and back, around British Columbia, and from August to October 1981 from Vancouver Island to the Maritimes. We concluded our cross-Canada trip by storing Dede near Halifax and flying to Germany for a visit, which opportunity led us to extend into a fourteen-year stay in my husband's hometown of Nuremberg.

For a long time we were sensible enough to value our steady incomes and social benefits, the company of friends and my husband's family, and all the quality, variety and stimulation Europe had to offer. Every couple of years we were content to come back to the Coast on a four-week holiday. Nevertheless we carried that first year and a half of simple, mobile living in Canada, and with it the urge to quit our jobs, break with routine and move back to the Islands, like a latent virus that flared up every now and then under the right conditions.

There had never been any question in either of our minds that we would return eventually to Canada's West Coast to live. The only blank we had to fill in was when. When we were older? *How much older?* When we had saved enough money? *How much was enough?* When the changes at work made our jobs less enjoyable? *How much less enjoyable?* When the time was right? *How right is right?*

We began to wonder if we didn't do it soon, would we end up like so many people, who keep shelving their dreams and desires until the kids (we have none) are finished their education, until the mortgage, loans and credit cards are paid off (we were debt-free), until various family or social obligations are met (ours were few and demanded little), and find ourselves too sick, too old, too tired or too tied down to budge. Wasn't it better, while we were in our early forties, still healthy and daring, to take a leap and risk falling on our faces than never to jump at all and wish in our old age that we had? After much deliberation and agonizing, we quit our jobs, disposed of most of our possessions, and came back to Canada in June of 1995.

We returned to the Southern Gulf Islands after a summer of visiting family in the West to look for a place where we could hole up, hunker down and indulge in our ideas and projects. The affordable properties we checked out on Salt Spring, Galiano, the Penders and Saturna Islands tended to be handyman specials that required on top of the proverbial TLC additional talent, labour and cash.

Just when we were beginning to think we'd exhausted the real estate market, we were introduced to a fellow on Mayne Island who happened, like us, to be making some changes in his life and had his place up for sale. The property was conveniently located within walking distance of the ferry terminal at Village Bay in a residential area on Wood Dale Drive that extended along the ridge toward Mount Parke. At the head of an inclining driveway, a wooden gate opened onto a narrow, level courtyard. At the far end sat a 1970's Silver Streak travel trailer that was largely concealed from the road below by a row of young cedars.

Abundantly wooded with mature arbutus, maple, fir and cedar trees, the usable part of the half-acre property had been cut out of the mountain slope. A nearly vertical bedrock bluff rose at a steep angle to its base, and ended at the top in an undisturbed talus slope that had formed over time by materials falling from the bluff. A vigorous climb through the woods along deer trails, rocky terraces and makeshift steps terminated in a wide-angle view of the Gulf Islands and Swanson Channel. On the upper, flatter moss-covered rock slope several metres below the crest and beyond the nearest neighbours we sat and gazed all the way to the ferry terminal at Swartz Bay on Vancouver Island and the Olympic Mountains in Washington State.

Of course this private little park came with its limitations. In real estate terminology the property was classified as recreational, which meant that permanent buildings over the size of one hundred square feet were not permitted. Because of the potentially unstable mountain ridge and the possibility of falling rocks and sliding materials during an earthquake or tremors, there was a covenant against all but the first few properties. We needed some time to think things over but, having no intentions to build a new cabin or make expensive or extensive improvements, we made an offer. Within a week the property was ours.

In September we moved in. The weather provided us with

mild sunny days in which to carry out our initial scouring and shining to bring the place up to our standards. While my husband took over the tall and heavy tasks such as scrubbing the ceiling and the exterior of the trailer, and re-organizing and re-shaping the yard, I tackled the interior cleaning and redecorating. Cushion and mattress covers sewn from floral-patterned upholstery cotton modernized the original 1970's decor and colour scheme. Enlarged prints from holidays on Crete disguised the tacky mirror tiles glued to the cupboard doors. After a couple of weeks we had the place clean, functional and funky.

The evenings were still mild enough for us to sit outside and take in our surroundings. In various large rocks cropping up around the yard we could perceive the faces of ancient guardian spirits, and the stars transformed the circular clearing of our yard into a "faery garden". Here we had found just the place where we could pursue the life of quiet introspection for which we had been longing.

As caretakers rather than cultivators, we intended to keep our property wild and natural, and welcomed any plant or animal that had already established itself in the yard. Spiders scurried out of various openings and built their sparkling webs wherever they could be anchored. Tree frogs climbed up to sit on the cool window ledges or the braces of the front awning of the trailer to escape the afternoon sun. A wire fence around the perimeter of the yard kept deer out of our living space, but we could often hear them foraging along the trails in our woods. When a mouse came snooping around while we were having our lunch outside, we could only guess who might show up next.

Bumps against the bottom of the trailer introduced us to a night visitor rummaging through the tin cans we'd been collecting in a plastic bag underneath for recycle. Occasionally we discovered a lid or two lying on one of the trails that led into the woods. We suspected a raccoon, and to entice our nocturnal guest into making regular appearances, we began setting out left-overs. Besides having a sizeable appetite, our guest was not fussy about cleaning up our latest special of noodles with garlic, mushroom and eggplant. As willing as it was to partake of our table scraps, the visitor remained reluctant to reveal its identity.

In the meantime we had become hosts to a company of busy black-hooded juncos, showy varied thrushes and high-spirited rufous-sided towhees. My husband had been spreading birdseed on the ground but, as winter approached and the competition for food grew with the number of guests, he left an additional helping in a home-made bird feeder which the previous owner had fastened to the gate above the driveway.

One early December afternoon a light snowfall dusted the ground like icing sugar on a pan of brownies. All of a sudden we saw a sturdy raccoon making its way toward the front fence. He easily mastered the climb up a driftwood fence post, then proceeded to straddle the two cedar shingles which formed the bird feeder's triangular roof and to lower himself so that he could reach the feed with one hand while managing with the other to keep from sliding or falling off. After grabbing a couple of handfuls, he had to pull himself up and re-adjust his purchase before he attempted to finish the job from another angle. Due as much to his persistence as to his agility, the culprit managed to scatter onto the ground what he couldn't gobble up. If we had had a video camera, our recording of the raid would surely have won first prize on *America's Funniest Home Videos*.

A further assault on the bird feeder, this time at night, ended with the crude construction lying in pieces on the ground. My husband dismantled the feeder, reinforced it and nailed it back up. The birds did not care to feed from the feeder, so to accommodate them and to prevent future raccoon vandalism he spread birdseed only on the ground. As for our furry friend, we figured that if he were going to become a regular, we should provide him with treats he would not have to take such risks to enjoy.

The empty plastic yogurt container we had been filling told us that Bandit, as we christened him, was still coming around on a regular basis. Eager for an encore to his premiere performance, we had to wait until winter settled in and natural food sources dwindled before Bandit began to show up during the day.

On the left-hand side of our yard a set of stone steps began a natural trail up and into the woods. Much of the trail was covered with a lush undergrowth of Oregon grape, salal and ferns, and several large rocks and stumps formed a perfect route for Bandit to enter our yard without being easily seen. Next to a large cedar tree lay a big old log which he used to make his sporadic entrances.

On Boxing Day we were surprised to look up from the breakfast table as two raccoons ambled onto the cedar gangway. Stopping just long enough for Bandit's ladyfriend, we assumed, to take a peek at his new night-spot, they turned and hurried off like Christmas holidayers hunting for Boxing Day bargains.

Chapter 2
Bandit and the Ladies

Our new life on Mayne Island was not really that new at all. Moving into a twenty-four-foot travel trailer was a logical continuation of the simple life we had led fifteen years earlier, and a step up in that we could now enjoy the luxuries of electricity and plumbing, running piped water, a two-way fridge and propane stove, a shower, a small television, a telephone and our own private yard. All we had to do was refine the skills we had continued to practise even during our affluent time in Germany, and make improvements wherever we could.

For the first while we did not want to work at any job. Since neither attractive nor lucrative employment opportunities were plentiful on an island the size of Mayne, we would have to rely on our own financial resources. This meant that our first principle would be to live simply. Before we left Germany, we had sold, discarded and given away whatever was not valuable, functional, durable and essential, and into six large suitcases we packed only those possessions which would be too costly to replace. After all, we did not want to start out by wasting any of our savings on having crates and trunks of stuff shipped across the Atlantic when there are plenty of stores on the other side.

To make sensible use of our small living space, we first sorted the clothes, tools, utensils, bedding and personal items we immediately needed from those we could store in our ten-by-ten-foot cedar shed or in the 1982 custom-camperized Chevy van we'd bought in July. (A previous owner, obviously a skilled carpenter, had lined the inside of the van with tongue-and-groove wood panelling and built in cupboards and a closet, all of which made the vehicle into a cozy travelling cabin.) After that we would make it a point on an on-going basis to evaluate our possessions with a sober, utilitarian eye and get rid of anything that served only to take up space.

Once we'd detached ourselves from our possessions, we were amazed and *relieved* to discover how many of them we really didn't need, would never use, and did not even miss once they were gone. Unlike people who believe that their quality of life advances with bigger, better, grander, and more property, we agree with H. D. Thoreau who wrote: "A man is rich in proportion to what he can do without."

The next principle we established after paring everything down was to make the most out of the little we had. This meant keeping the space, including our outhouse, clean, comfortable and attractive. Trailers, RV's and campers, and even cabins can quickly turn into doghouses when the owners do not take even the minimal time that is required to keep the place clean. Our concept of unconventional living does not include living in squalor; if I want to take the untrodden path, then I believe in doing so with dignity and in style.

While living in a small space and on a frugal budget forced us to choose between the things we could and couldn't do without, living on an island left us no choice but to forgo the urban amenities that most people believe to be indispensable. With a permanent population in 1995 of over eight hundred, Mayne Island had two general stores (a year later a third grocery store opened in the Mayne Street Mall), a bakery, a hardware and building supplies centre, a gas station, and a postal outlet. While we could buy our basic groceries in the "village" at Miners Bay, I always had to take into account when I made my shopping list that a few items might be unavailable or cost more than we were willing to pay.

To do our laundry, banking and major shopping once a month we took the Gulf Islands ferry to Salt Spring Island, where we had lived and married fourteen years earlier. The ferry left Village Bay before noon and arrived at Long Harbour around one o'clock p.m. Rather than rushing around to get everything done in time to catch the three-thirty p.m. ferry back, we preferred to make our trip into a leisurely overnight camping event. We stayed in Ruckle Park, where we had camped one winter in our first step van, and combined our chores with a visit to our dear ninety-five-year-old friend and adopted second Mom, Alma Williams, in the senior citizens' housing.

Because we were living on a fixed income that amounted to an eighth of what we had been earning in Germany, we planned and recorded our purchases, made shopping lists and *looked at them*, compared prices and bargains at the two main grocery stores in Ganges, Salt Spring's business centre, and bought larger quantities of essential items when they were on sale. When tempted to buy something, we always asked ourselves: do we need this, do we need it now or can we wait, do we already have something that would do the trick, or can we come up with a more cost-efficient solution?

Although we were frugal, we did treat ourselves to a burger or wings and beer at the pub, and in the morning breakfast at our favourite café. After all, our modest way of life was neither a mission we were pursuing with single-minded zeal nor a regimen we adhered to with military pride. Practising financial restraint didn't preclude the purchase of a radio-CD player, either. Of the many things we could live without, the pleasures of listening to our CD collection and CBC radio were not among them!

Loaded down with supplies and exhausted from the city that Salt Spring had become in comparison to Mayne Island, we were always glad to get back home and resume our pet projects. My husband liked to putt around in the yard or climb through the woods and investigate the upper talus slope, and I worked on my writing. Our own best company, we always did our shopping together and went for walks in the neighbourhood or to Dinner Bay park on a dry afternoon.

After having been away for almost fourteen years, we watched the evening news on t.v. to catch up on the Canadian political scene, and it was with distress and disappointment that we found that we'd come back to yet another referendum in Quebec. Discriminating television viewers, we regularly watched the news and a few comedy and drama series that became our favourites. Most of the time we retired early to the comfort of the pull-out king-sized bed we'd fashioned across the width of the trailer with a plywood insert, and read—voluminously and voraciously—from the eclectic stacks of the Mayne Island Library.

Knowing how capricious West Coast weather can be, we had decided when we bought our place to stick it out over the winter and take the wet and gloomy with the beautiful and balmy. During windstorms that hurled pine cones onto our roof like savages attacking us from above, we were only too aware of the thin aluminium shell that sheltered us from the elements. Our trailer was not winterized to withstand extreme cold, so we always watched the weather forecast to prepare for the next Pineapple Express (named after the warm moisture-laden fronts that move in from Hawaii) or icy Arctic outflow winds.

Letting the weather determine our activities may not sound like fun or freedom, but we adapted and became so organized, disciplined and conscious of what we did and how we did it that in the process we freed ourselves of habits that no longer served us. It was no great hindrance, for instance, to dash out to the outhouse in the morning rain or to plan our cooking, showering and shopping around possible rain showers. When the power went out, as it did frequently for a few hours during a storm and usually toward evening, we made our bed and crawled under our down duvet until we fell asleep or the power came back on.

We had an electric ceramic heater for the front and a baseboard heater for the back, but unchecked condensation inside the trailer could collect into an ugly problem if we didn't stay on top of it. Already we'd scrubbed and scoured as far as our hands could reach to get rid of mould and mildew on hidden surfaces and in dark corners. As soon as the sun shone—and on the West Coast the sun always comes out again and you forget that it ever rained—we opened the windows and door, and aired out.

A sudden cold snap in January caught us unprepared when -10°C temperatures froze our water. Luckily there was no damage to our water pipes and no leaks or mess when the weather warmed up, but we'd had to get water from private sources and stretch it for five days. To avert such negligence in future we planned to always keep a twenty-litre container of water in the shed.

On our shopping trips we hadn't yet found a suitable non-electric heat source, a clear must, but we managed to stay warm and cozy inside the trailer. Like sturdy perennials hardened to their surroundings, we never once came down with the usual winter cold or flu that we used to catch so easily in stuffy overheated buildings and public transportation in Germany. In fact we felt healthier, lighter and less stressed than we had for some time, and we endured winter's tests without complaint or regret.

Having consciously removed ourselves from the solid structures that shield society from the forces of Nature, we sometimes felt like modern pioneers. I would be taking myself much too seriously if I failed to use the qualifier "modern" since although we had scaled down our financial and material needs to far below what the average North American might consider adequate, we were still far better off than any of our forefathers and foremothers, and much more fortunate than millions of poor, homeless and jobless folk who have to get through every day on greater ingenuity, forbearance, and faith than we practised.

In all we were content and grateful to be doing what we wanted to, and the simplest pleasures gave us the greatest joy. One of these was naturally a visit from Bandit.

We had not seen Bandit or his ladyfriend since Boxing Day, and the January cold snap and snowfall had kept them away during the day. The growls and snarls, scuffles and scrapes in the woods accompanied in the background by the throbbing high voltage chorus of mating tree frogs alerted us to antics in the woods at night. Reminiscent more of acts of aggression than forms of courtship, this lusty ruckus carried on into February.

When temperatures returned to seasonal levels, Bandit strolled one afternoon across the upper terrace of our yard with a companion. Inclined only to pass through during the day as if on a reconnaissance mission, Bandit preferred to drop in around sunset when we made supper left-overs available. He blended so perfectly into the rocky surroundings that we had to be vigilant, and lucky, to catch sight of him. He usually came alone, but when accompanied by a date, she had to wait, petulantly of course, on the side until he'd had his share. Although we could not always see our visitors come and go, we could hear them growling at each other in front of our trailer.

A raccoon's relationship with its mate, we learned, was a shallow affair. After only a few dates, Bandit started making solo appearances just around newstime. Soon his bachelor routine and meal were interrupted by a newcomer, whose submissive pose suggested that she was a female. She was too skinny to be one of Bandit's former consorts, and her bedraggled look led us to assume that she was a young orphan. At first we called her Sweetie, then Snoopy after her habit of turning over, sniffing at and checking out almost everything in our yard. Eventually we settled on Foxy after we watched her back up into Bandit's face and slide herself onto the food dish.

A second time while Bandit was eating on a broad, flat stump in the garden, Foxy sidled up to a bordering piece of driftwood, lounged against it for a while, then edged herself upward so that, with her tail lifted, she gained access to the dinner table. To our surprise Bandit backed off and moved on. After a series of more stressful encounters, Foxy timed her visits to circumvent the Big Boy, and Bandit generally came early enough to fill his stomach rather than fight with a little tramp.

Instead of putting food out before Bandit and Foxy came, my husband waited until they arrived so that they would come to recognize the hand that fed them. He had changed the fare to dry cat food, and moved the food dish to the foot of the stone steps where Bandit was accustomed to making his entrances and exits. Bandit's first reaction when my husband came out of the trailer was to back up the stone steps and wait at a safe distance while food was being dished out in the cedar shed where we stored it.

Exceptionally excitable, Foxy first ran around the garden or up the stone steps to the top landing behind the big arbutus tree. There she stood up, bear-like, on a rock and stretched her skinny body so that she could observe her waiter when he emerged with her order. No matter how hungry or eager Bandit and Foxy were, they would not come down from their perch until my husband had retreated. It wasn't until summer that they overcame their wariness.

The new location gave our raccoons more elbow room when they happened to show up at the same time, and it allowed us to observe them better from our wrap-around front windows. Eventually Bandit and Foxy came to tolerate each other. Of the entire nine-member cast who entertained us over the summer, they were the only ones who got along.

Used to the rare security of our food bank, Bandit and Foxy changed their routines to accommodate earlier and longer stays, and sometimes they'd hang around for a digestive pause. Frequently they would position themselves on one of the stone steps, and sit and stare toward the window of the trailer with such intensity that we had to wonder who was observing whom. At times they would clean and groom themselves or, later as they became more trusting, they would have a short snooze.

On those occasions when Bandit or Foxy took a notion to sit still, which was never for long, I would try my hand at drawing them. These amateur attempts taught me to pick out details that later helped us distinguish one raccoon from the other with considerable accuracy.

One of my favourite quotes about wild animals comes from Annie Dillard's *Pilgrim at Tinker Creek*, in which she writes: "The great hurrah about wild animals is that they exist at all, and the greater hurrah is the actual moment of seeing them." To this I would add that the greatest hurrah is the chance to get to know them. We took every opportunity to study each animal's physical characteristics, which we tried to capture by choosing a suitable name, and to acquaint ourselves with the preferences and habits that expressed their personalities. And distinct characters they were!

Although he'd made a larcenous first impression when he raided the bird feeder in December, Bandit's round ears and pudgy face lent him a Winnie the Pooh appeal. He boasted a sizeable appetite (which made him no anomaly) and, if he kept eating like he did, we feared that the steep slopes, big rocks and high stumps over and around which he had to navigate would soon become a major challenge. It was hard to judge his age (a raccoon's average life span is ten to twelve years), but we assumed that he must have a few good years on his back. These he carried with dignity and authority.

As fox-like in her features as she was in her demeanour, Foxy remained for all she devoured a skinny little oddball with a ratty tail bent at the end like a pipe cleaner. Usually she scooped her food out of the dish with her left hand, a habit which made us wonder if raccoons might be left- or right-handed. In addition to exhibiting eccentric eating habits, she would take frantic shortcuts through our herbs and plants. When we were sitting out in the yard in the afternoon, she would sneak in from somewhere and lie on the stone steps, or climb a tree and look down at us until we noticed her.

Now, when an eating establishment offers prompt service, consistent quality and a homey atmosphere, word—or scent—is bound to travel. In March our next patron, another female, turned up for a late brunch. She had a toe missing on her left hind foot and a nick in her left ear, and on account of her tattered appearance I named her Raggedy Ann. Her first few appearances did not attract much notice. She was about the same size as Bandit, so we tended to confuse the two until on one occasion she upset the freshly filled water dish, attacked the empty food dish, and absconded with it into the woods.

Accustomed to leaving unambiguous messages, Raggedy Ann tolerated us coming within a foot of her. When my husband presented her food, she backed up no farther than the first stone step, then came right back down to dig into the goodies.

One day he decided to test if our newest guest was really more trusting than Bandit and Foxy, or less patient. Stepping up to the raised plateau where he had been leaving food, he squatted down, sprinkled a few cheerios of dry cat food into his hand, and held them out to her. Raggedy backed up into the garden, sneaked down under and around the small fir trees, crawled toward his hand, then retreated, all the while carrying on her wriggly, testing "do-I-dare-do-I-not, gee-I'd-sure-like-to-but-there's-just-no-way-I-can" dance until she finally planted herself and stretched her arms as far as they could reach.

With her black eyes fixed on my husband the whole time, she overcame herself just long enough to scoop up a few pellets. With each helping she shortened the steps of her ritual dance, as if it were against her principles to be too easy-to-get. I don't know for which of the two the experience was the greater conquest, but right then and there Raggedy gained access to my husband's heart, and she was to show more often than not that she had his number!

Raggedy was the only one who ever ate out of our hands. She would have eaten off our plates, she would have moved into our trailer and thrown us out, if we had let her! More domineering than a mother-in-law, more charming than a diva, more brazen than a hussy, more pushy than a super shopper, more cunning than a gypsy, more wicked than a witch, more unpredictable than a hurricane, more irresistible than Belgian chocolates, and more loveable than a stuffed toy, this girl was not be overlooked! I couldn't help but picture her as a slightly slovenly dame who didn't think twice about rushing out to the supermarket in her bathrobe and curlers just to satisfy her slightest craving.

By spring our observations and the raccoon's regular contact established Bandit, Foxy and Raggedy Ann as individuals. However, if one of them had not been around for awhile or came when it was almost dark, we could not always identify them with absolute certainty. In moments of doubt their individual eating habits proved to be their most reliable calling card. Foxy scooped out her food with her left hand; Bandit often tipped over the yogurt dish when he was finished; and Raggedy, well she was just Raggedy!

Chapter 3
A Full House

Our intention from the moment we took possession of our property was to keep our yard in a natural state so that it would continue to attract animals and birds. Any gardening we might do, considering our limited experience in raising plants and vegetables, would be mostly experimental and, despite the lot's southern exposure, likely subject to failure given the dry, rocky and not very fertile soil.

My husband's first project that early spring was to lay a flagstone walk from the trailer to the shed using large rocks, which he dug up or dislodged from around the yard. As well as adding some sophistication to the place, the walkway made it easier to go from the trailer to the shed and the outhouse after a typical West Coast rain had saturated the ground.

Next we plotted out a small terrace where we wanted to plant a few hardy herbs and flowers, and dug up space in front of the trailer for a mini-lawn. Breaking up the ground by hand bent a few tools and made the muscles in my hands as stiff and sore as if I'd spent a day clearing an ice-packed sidewalk. Before the patch was ready to seed, we had to pick out pailfuls and pailfuls of rocks and stones. There were still enough pailfuls in the ground, I swore, to build a stone wall around the place. In any case we wouldn't have problems with drainage! Once the lawn was seeded, our work was far from done as my husband had to nurse and protect the new grass from the robins who liked to dig around for worms.

Between purchases of seeds and a few eclectic bedding plants at the local Home Hardware, and an assortment of freebies from acquaintances, we managed to get a reasonable start on our garden. Our only edibles were a rhubarb plant which would need at least a year until we could harvest it, a meagre row of beans, and some lettuce and radishes, which grew more to our amusement than to our sustenance. I had no high hopes, but was curious nevertheless to see the results and willing to learn lessons for the next growing season.

In the meantime we decided to fly to Germany for five weeks in May and June. Besides visiting family and friends, we had a couple of matters we wanted to take care of. When I resigned from my teaching job, I set things up with the language school where I had been employed so that I could return after a year if I wanted to. Now, one short year later, we discovered that it was much too soon to step right back into our former life.

Of course all that we had enjoyed while living in

Nuremberg—the company of family and friends, afternoons in a beer garden, a trip to the Alps—were all as pleasurable as ever. Over the course of our visit, however, we felt as if we were looking from the outside into the window of a house we used to live in. Although all the rooms were furnished and arranged the way we had left them, the place no longer seemed to belong to us. Or I should say, we no longer belonged to the place.

Our original decision to move back to Canada had meant more to us than taking an extended holiday or dropping out for a few months until we got bored or restless. What we wanted to do was to change our life, and this giant step required us to give in whole-heartedly to our dreams—*or our demons*—and to be committed to taking the time to succeed or fail. After only a year on Mayne Island there was still a lot we'd have to get out of our system before we could ever considering going back to what we'd had. Besides, we had our fledgling garden to tend to, and of course our raccoons.

Since Bandit's first appearance in December, followed by Foxy's in February and Raggedy Ann's in March, our raccoons' daily visits had become more of an event than anything that could have happened in the news. We had become so attached to them, in fact, that our greatest concern while we were away was not whether we would return to find our trailer intact and our plants alive, but if our raccoons would still come around.

As if she had already sensed that we were back, little Foxy showed up the evening of our return. Our second guest the following day was neither Bandit nor Raggedy, but a pretty, dark female who sat like a chipmunk with her belly exposed while she munched on her food with the relish of a true connoisseur. A clean, orderly girl with a preference for dipping her food or her hands in the water dish, our newcomer became known as Putzi, which in German is a common name for a pet and, coming from the verb *putzen* (to clean), denotes something cute or adorable. Although Putzi's washing turned out to be only a temporary thing, her name stuck.

According to my reading, raccoons do not actually wash their food; rather they immerse it in water to increase their tactile sensations.

Four regular raccoons required a cheaper food supply so we switched to dry dog food which could also be bought in larger quantities. As the pieces of food were formed for larger canine jaws, the raccoons reminded me of little kids trying to chew on jawbreakers. Except for Raggedy of course who would unceremoniously grab and devour, Bandit, Foxy and Putzi would pick up a piece and roll it vigorously between their hands before taking a bite. This idiosyncrasy was the source of constant amusement, especially later in the summer when we had a yard full of raccoons and Bandit, who found nothing to eat, would come up to the large rocks in front of the screen door and put on a pantomime by rubbing his empty hands together.

In addition to watching our raccoons use their silver-gloved hands to scoop, roll, hold and turn their food, we were amused by the grunting, sighing and smacking which confirmed their obvious concentration and delight. Their table manners were not exemplary, but they would occasionally hold their hands under their mouths or in front to catch the crumbs that flew out as their teeth and jaws pulverized each crunchy clump of dog food.

Like fugitives who expect to be apprehended at any moment, they were not able to enjoy their meal with complete abandon. While their fingers scoured the ground for food, their black eyes and white-tipped ears were constantly checking for danger.

By now our place had definitely become *the* fast food outlet in the neighbourhood, and Bandit, Foxy, Raggedy and Putzi kept my husband, their loyal waiter, hopping. Characteristically unsociable, they preferred to travel and dine alone, but just as we had been observing them with avid interest, it turned out that they had been scrutinizing each other with even keener eyes.

Whereas Bandit tended to be dignified and reserved, the females, in particular Raggedy Ann, carried on when it came to crunchy (which is what we had begun to call the dog food) like bad-tempered little kids who, seeing that one has got some goodies, demand their share, too. Due to Raggedy's plastic fetish (she'd already demolished a couple of yogurt containers) and the frequency with which two raccoons tried to monopolize the dish, we decided to dispense with dinnerware and leave the food on the ground.

Despite our peace-keeping strategy, conflicts inevitably

broke out. First our guests would growl, then snap and lunge at each other until one submitted with a whimper or a retreat. Often their squabbling would continue until my husband went outside and gave each its separate portion. Generally his democratic approach worked, and, unless bad behaviour justified the temporary withdrawal of service, everyone went away satisfied. If not, well, they just sorted things out in their own furious but harmless way.

One mid-summer night we were about to go to bed when, because of the full moon, we noticed Foxy sitting right next to the trailer and begging below the window. My husband went out with a snack that he sometimes kept inside the trailer for off-hours traffic, and saw that Bandit was waiting as well by the stone steps. While they fed, Bandit and Foxy seemed to quiver and pulsate in the moonlight, as if they were players in an electrified midsummer night's dream.

Bandit and Foxy staged their next evening performance after sharing a relatively civilized meal. Stretching themselves out on the stone steps above the garden, they reclined like Antony and Cleopatra. At this point Putzi, still a wary newcomer, had slipped into our yard from the opposite end and lay crouched on one of the higher shelves. While she sussed out the situation from a distance, Bandit and Foxy regarded her every move, and growled as if to say, "What does *she* want here?" Raccoons, however, are not easily deterred by threats or insults, and Putzi demonstrated her raccoon determination to have her turn at the supper table by lying low and hanging in there until Bandit and Foxy had left the building.

After that night, we referred to the rectangular plateau below the stone steps as the garden stage. With a summer theatre right in our yard, we were in store for a series of comedies and dramas we wouldn't have missed for front row seats at a Three Tenors concert!

Although Foxy had initially stood up to Bandit and had even outsmarted him a couple of times, she was no match for Raggedy Ann or Putzi in either size or temperament, and her status slipped to that of under-raccoon. Once after a loud racket in one of the cedar trees with an unidentified opponent, she came tearing down as if her skinny tail had been set on fire. She had shown up a couple of times with minor scratches, and after this particular incident she came infrequently and only later in the evening. When she did venture into the yard for a late evening treat, she'd steal up to the trailer in her harried fashion or climb up on the rocks and peer at the screen door.

My husband did manage to coax Foxy away from the garden stage to the other end of the yard where there were more trees to climb and, just in case, a couple of exits into the woods. That way she could have her snack in relative peace, but with the other raccoons on constant look-out for a hand-out, we could not guarantee Foxy her privacy. Once Putzi, who had already had more than her share, returned just as Foxy was settling down to her late evening snack. Doggedly Putzi tried to move in on Foxy's pile and, although we didn't usually interfere, we couldn't stand by and let poor

Foxy be intimidated. We felt badly about chasing Putzi off, but as we learned, a raccoon does not bear grudges.

Apart from the fact that we provided free meals and a safe environment for our friends to feed, play and relax, we thought that there had to be something else about our particular location that attracted as many raccoons as it did. Perhaps there might be some kind of natural birthing ground in our vicinity. The woods were full of mature trees, decaying stumps, cavernous rocks and mossy hideaways where a mother raccoon might bear and shelter her kits until they were ready to go out into the world.

Judging by our females' voracious appetites and the frequency of their visits, we were curious to find out which of our three girls might be a mother. If they felt so at home, surely they would bring their young!

Chapter 4
Ricky, Rocky and the Three Racketeers

With the bulk of our yard work behind us and only a few touch-up painting projects scheduled for inside the trailer, we were free to relish our first jobless summer. While we were employed, we never joined the masses in their summer exodus southward, and preferred to stay around home and hike in the country on the weekends. Of course there were no beer gardens or country inns to hike to on Mayne Island like there were in the countryside surrounding Nuremberg, but there were bays, beaches and parks to explore. Our greatest luxury was that we could go where we wanted when we felt like it and stay as long as we cared.

On the night of the summer solstice we returned home from a picnic party to the serendipitous smells and sounds of the season. For a few minutes we lingered under the stars and listened to night's lullaby when a warbling we could not associate with any bird or creature issued from the upper woods. Figuring we would have the opportunity to identify it another time, we turned in.

A couple of weeks later we were sitting outside after supper when we heard that same warbling accompanied by some rustling in our neighbour's woods. I stood up just in time to spot a small masked face peering through the deer fence. We held our breaths while the mother, we hoped, climbed into our yard, but we had to wait another week before Raggedy Ann suddenly appeared on Bandit's big cedar log with a kitten-sized baby behind her. She seemed about to come down to the garden stage when a frantic cooing in the woods turned into a high-pitched shrieking, and in a flash she took off with her kit scurrying behind her.

A few days later while we were doing the supper dishes, a loud chorus of cooing announced activity again on the big cedar log. Lined up side by side this time were *three* raccoon babies! Immediately we slipped out of the trailer and slid onto the bench outside the door. The three kits continued to wail and sing while Raggedy Ann, we assumed, checked to see if the coast was clear. When *Putzi* appeared at the top of the stone steps, we had the explanation to her recent appetite and aggressive behaviour toward Foxy! When Putzi whistled, all three kits slid, tumbled and bounced down the steep stone steps to the garden stage where they huddled tightly around their mother.

Now, cute may be a word that is scorned in literary circles and over-used in colloquial language, but I can think of no better one for baby raccoons with their spiky ringed tails, shoe button eyes, and blunt noses with the smudge of a mask that makes them look as if they've been playing make-up artist with Dad's shoe cream. Breathlessly we watched their investigations for awhile, then wondered if a tasty treat might encourage their mother to let us enjoy them for a little longer. We hated to risk scaring them off, but my husband took a chance and glided towards them with a dish of food.

At first the three kits scooted for cover and dived into the salal, but at Putzi's signal they emerged and collected around her. The dog food, like the stone steps, was almost too big for them to handle, and the two larger kits succeeded in spitting out more than they could chew or swallow. All three showed keen interest in the Rubbermaid water container my husband had set out recently on the garden stage. After hoisting themselves up onto the rim of the container like children climbing monkey bars, they see-sawed and dipped their noses into the water, which they drank as it dripped into their mouths. Their visit had made our day, and we could hardly wait for the next one.

One beautiful Saturday afternoon in early August, that my husband and I fondly remember as Big Baby Day, we happened to be sitting front row centre in a shady spot under the big-leaf maple tree near the garden stage when Putzi appeared with her family. I was not sure how Putzi would react to our being so close, but she looked straight at us and only growled. Her warning was not intended to threaten us, as we soon came to understand, but to keep her babies in line. This time they stayed for over an hour, and my husband was able to take our first baby pictures.

We found it odd that Putzi, our most recent and reserved customer, should be the first to entrust us with her young. From Raggedy's earlier appearance on the cedar log with a kit, we knew that she had young ones, and when she stood up, she was clearly lactating. It was so unlike our audacious Raggedy to keep her babies a secret when there was little, if anything, in the way of desires that she ever hid from us. In any case she proved herself much better at extorting us with her mischief than we were at bribing her with food to bring her young.

That same Saturday Raggedy Ann must have realized that Putzi was upstaging her because shortly after Putzi left with her young, Raggedy paraded across the garden stage with twins. Her two were a size smaller and probably two or three weeks younger than Putzi's three. Timidly they tagged after their mother, who came straight up to us and demanded the reward we had promised her for delivering the goods. The twins were too small to be interested in dog food, but like their cousins they tested the water in the Rubbermaid container with their button noses, and played or snooped around the garden stage until Raggedy led them away.

While continuing to slip out in the morning for a quick breakfast on her own, Putzi honoured us with her young only sporadically at first. When my husband approached the garden stage with a family-sized helping of food, the three kits would flee up the steps, scatter into the salal or head up a tree, their favourite refuge, until they learned, and it didn't take long, that the Crunchy Man was not to be feared.

From Joan Ward-Harris's descriptions of her Vixen's three babies in *Creature Comforts*, I guessed Putzi's babies to be two females and a male and named them Molly, Dolly and Bugsy, the Three Racketeers. Bugsy, the smallest, was not as greedy or pushy as his two sisters, and he preferred to retreat to the steps and gnaw on his food in private. Molly, a miniature replica of Putzi, was scrappier than easy-going Dolly, and she crouched on the garden stage and growled whenever mother or sibling came near her pile of goodies.

When they were not busy eating, the Racketeers investigated the garden, pulled on the bright red star-shaped nicotiana flowers and let them bounce back up, or grappled with the ice plants as if they were knots that had to be untied. They stuck their hands into the various cracks and crevices between the stones and rocks to fish for goodies, turned over an assortment of sea shells to check out the underside, and peeked into the empty flower pots sitting on one of the stone steps. I was always expecting one of them to fall headfirst into a pot, or topple over with it, but none ever did, a fact which was probably due more to luck than skill.

Putzi carried out the duties of a single mom with thorough dedication. We could imagine that before she took her kits out she made sure that their hair was combed, their faces washed, their shoes shined and their shirts tucked in because they always looked and behaved like three little angels on their way to Sunday school. The only bad marks they would have received on their report cards would have been for their table manners, which they came by honestly.

Mealtimes were a free-for-all. Everyone stepped on whoever squatted in the way, and no one was the least apologetic when he or she happened to back up into the other one's face. Usually the Racketeers gathered around Putzi in a furry clump, and when one wanted to move, the best available route was over bodies. Their favourite way to secure their share of food was to sit on it. No matter how much they had under them or in front, they invariably reached over to sample someone else's serving. Growling at each other came naturally, and they had no compunction about growling at their mother, who growled right back.

With their active schedule, the Racketeers kept their mother going full tilt. Sometimes Putzi would remove herself to the side of the garden stage and space out while Molly, Dolly and Bugsy squabbled over their breakfast. A few times her head bobbed like a weary worker's on the bus ride home, and her body sagged and slumped until she came within millimetres of keeling over. The only break Putzi seemed to get before she led the Racketeers off on their excursions was when Molly held up the crew to finish the last crumbs or take one more drink.

Raggedy did not bring the twins very often at first because toddlers cramped her style. As my husband later discovered on one of his hikes up to the top of the talus slope, she had her den conveniently located in the woods right above our yard so that when the twins were napping she could easily slip down for snacks.

Having made our place her home away from home,

Raggedy was in and out all the time. As summer heated up, she came around for extended stays, and she liked to stand in the water container and cool off, especially after we exchanged it for a larger one that made a handy paddling pool. Occasionally she would lounge on a cool, flat rock and show more interest in what we were doing than in what her babies might be up to.

It would be unkind of me to suggest that just because she didn't seem to take Ricky and Rocky very far from home she was a lazy or negligent mother. In any case, her methods were consistent with her personality, and taking full advantage of her maternal status, she begged and bugged until we succumbed and handed out another treat.

When Raggedy brought Ricky and Rocky, they would often hide under the trailer or in the front garden, or play between the driftwood and the cedar hedge that screened our trailer from the street. When they felt neglected, they would coo loudly. With a low growl Raggedy would instruct the twins to stay where they were while she took off after my husband and followed him to the shed. At all times babies took a back seat to food!

Into late August Ricky and Rocky accompanied Raggedy on a steady basis. Rocky was a feisty vixen who was developing into a clone of her mother. At mealtimes she sat on the biggest pile of food and, crouching close to the ground, she growled and lunged with the tenacity of a tiger at any animal that came too close. If by chance she ran out of food first, she stole from her mother.

Ricky, who was a half-size smaller than Rocky, tended to be a little dreamer. Very early he gave the impression of a raccoon angel who didn't really belong to the wild world he'd been born into. He was forever lingering in the woods or wandering off alone, and would resort to loud cooing to attract attention. Most of the time Raggedy carried on eating or harassing the other guests who happened to be in the yard, and let Ricky cry until the call became a desperate wailing that even the coolest mother could not ignore.

Despite the twin's distinct personalities, they were their own best playmates. If we could not watch them, as we did one day when they spent most of the afternoon in the yard romping and frolicking with each other like kittens, we could often hear them cackling, cooing and chortling in the woods behind our place.

If Bandit happened to be around (and he did not let all this activity go unnoticed), we had to chase him off with the garden hose so that he couldn't intimidate the babies. Of course he didn't appreciate this sort of treatment, but Bandit didn't let our interventions get in the way of what he wanted, even if it meant that he had to come back later.

Bringing up the next generation fell entirely upon Putzi and Raggedy. When it came to child support, Bandit was a deadbeat Dad who regarded his offspring with hostility and annoyance. He never harmed the little ones, but went out of his way to show them his least accommodating side. They, in turn, regarded him with suspicion and deference, and their mothers made sure they stayed out of his way.

Raggedy's casual methods of childrearing suggested that she was the more experienced mother. Confident of her ability to strike like a B-52 bomber, she defended her portion of food more vigorously than she kept track of poor Ricky who was apt to linger in the woods or wander off by himself. When both families happened to be around at the same time and Ricky started wailing, it was Putzi who raised her head and rushed over until she realized that the cry-baby did not belong to her.

Keeping curious young raccoons in line required a mother's constant communication. Putzi and Raggedy delivered their warnings and instructions in a language which ranged from growling, whistling, whimpering to cooing. In response the kits cooed, warbled, chortled and trilled, producing an amazing repertoire of expressions. In addition to using their voices, their mothers' versatile hands were quick to hold their kits back or to steer them in the right direction.

When it came to discipline, our raccoon mothers were no push-overs. One sunny afternoon Raggedy was relaxing in the water container we now called their pool while the twins were climbing in and out, or snooping for crumbs on the garden stage. As precocious as her mother, Rocky was making a nuisance of herself when Raggedy reached over the side of the pool and gave her a good swat. Neither Raggedy nor Putzi had to resort to corporal punishment often, but when necessary, they wasted no time.

It was to Putzi's credit that the Racketeers travelled as

such a tight unit. The affection with which mother and kits related to each other was touching indeed. Bugsy in particular stayed close to Putzi, and while Molly and Dolly were busy climbing the trees near the big cedar log after breakfast, Putzi would vigorously clean him. A few times I caught sight of Bugsy reaching up and touching Putzi's nose, as if to give her a kiss. An egalitarian mother, she always gave the girls a thorough grooming when they came back down from the trees.

Tree climbing lessons were a riot, especially when at first the kits were not able to come down as quickly as they could go up. Instead of descending headfirst, they would slide downwards until it was safe to turn around and jump off. Soon, however, they mastered the art of climbing down headfirst, and they graduated from fir and cedar trees to the trickier arbutus near the stone steps. For a short time the shingled roof of our cedar storage shed served as a testing ground for their climbing skills, and we could hear them skittering around on top when we went in to get something.

Our big arbutus tree proved the ideal place for fun, especially when all three Racketeers were up there at once. It didn't take them long to discover the plastic rope that my husband had attached to support a long drooping branch on the big leaf maple below. After watching the whole branch wave and shake in the air one morning as if caught in a fierce windstorm, I walked over to discover one little masked bandit up in the crotch of the tree, holding the rope in his teeth and having a furious tug-of-war.

Our young raccoons were learning quickly, and as skilled imitators they'd taken to accompanying their mothers on their race with my husband to the shed. Given the right opportunity they'd all have been in there like dirty shirts. Therefore we always kept our shed closed and padlocked when we went away.

On the whole our five raccoon babies were well-behaved. Their worst misdemeanour was digging in the lawn, or racing through the flowers and herbs. If they knocked something over, dug a hole in the grass or roughed up a plant, we could never be angry for long at those masked innocents peeking out of the undergrowth. More of a game than any earnest attempt to control their inclinations, our scolding resulted in their scrambling up a tree, ducking behind a log or diving into the salal.

With the exception of the lawn into which we'd put a lot of energy, we weren't growing anything in our garden that the Racketeers or the twins could destroy. And if a few plants fell victim to their play, well, the rare experience we knew we were fortunate to have more than made up for any losses.

Chapter 5
Close Encounters

Over the summer Ricky and Rocky, and the Three Racketeers had been receiving most of the applause on the garden stage, but they did not completely upstage the starring adults, who were as capable as ever of putting on their own stellar performances.

Our leading lady Raggedy Ann was making her grand appearances at least two or three times a day. As intelligent as she was impatient, she had taken to following my husband to the shed like a dog. When he slipped through the door, she dived into the crawl space under the shed. She would then turn around and poke her head out so that she could see exactly when he emerged with dinner. In a more playful mood she sometimes climbed one of the trees between the shed and the compost box, and waited with her head poised at her faithful servant's eye level.

In the early spring my husband had put up a post with a small shelf next to the trailer where I could leave a pot of noodles to cool outside. By keeping an extra portion of dog food on the shelf in summer, he saved himself an extra trip to the shed when guest after guest arrived in rapid succession. On her second or third round already and not entitled to further, let alone immediate, service, Raggedy would wander over from the garden stage, sniff out the trailer deck, reach up to the shelf and knock off the container so that she could help herself. In case Raggedy upset a pot of hot noodles, or attempted something equally dangerous, we stopped leaving anything out on the post.

Ever hopeful, she continued to return to the site, and in the process of checking it out, discovered the screen door, which we always left open in warm weather. When I was cooking in the afternoon, Raggedy would come up to the screen and peer in, as if she expected me to open the door for her. If I had, she wouldn't have hesitated to barge right in, snatch the wooden spoon out of my hand and take over the kitchen.

When my husband was working in the yard, she'd come up to him and tug on his pant leg. When we were sitting outside, she would boldly approach. In case neither of us jumped up and dashed to the shed for food, she would reach out and scratch our shoes.

Early one morning before we were even up, Raggedy climbed up on one of the front propane tanks. Balancing herself in front of the kitchen window, she nosed up to the glass to see what the hell was the big hold-up in there, didn't we know what time it was! The sight of Raggedy staring into our window was a masterpiece! The second time she tried this, I had only a hasty opportunity to snap a picture of her, which unfortunately did not turn out.

We had to give Raggedy credit for ingenuity and bravado, but we could not encourage her antics, as we knew full well that more mischief would follow. By placing slippery, unstable objects around the propane tank, my husband managed to thwart her voyeurism; which was when, incorrigible and inventive, she began to climb up on the rocks beside our trailer and position herself so that she and her twins were the first thing we saw when I sat up and opened the bedroom curtain in the morning!

Despite her charm, we did not find everything Raggedy Ann did cute and amusing. The "mutt", as we began calling her, quickly figured out that when all else failed she could extort more food out of my husband by digging around in the lawn. At one point she got so carried away, despite the extra food she'd already connived out of us, that I tried chasing her off with a broom. While Ricky and Rocky scooted up a tree, Raggedy grumbled and huffed (she literally did!) like a grievously offended aunt as she retreated up the steps and into the woods.

Right away of course she came back down and resumed her nonsense. After a few fruitless efforts to teach Raggedy manners, we decided to dispense with the broom altogether. Sooner or later she would tire of the lawn strategy, we figured, and come up with a new ploy.

The damage she'd done to our lawn was more cosmetic

than structural anyway, and in the end we had no alternative but to forgive her for being the loveable rascal that she was. Besides, how can you punish a wild animal for doing exactly what Nature has programmed it to do, and who carries on at your own invitation?

Although Raggedy had established herself as the show stopper, Bandit was putting on some outstanding performances of his own. For most of the summer our leading man had arranged his schedule to assure maximum privacy and minimum conflict. But as the appearances of his offspring increased, Bandit found himself forced to share the stage with a company of amateurs who had neither the courtesy to ask if they could join in nor the manners to wait off-stage until he had made his exit.

The moments where he could stretch out and groom himself or curl up on the stone steps and have a nap after his evening meal were few and far between. If he was lucky, he could dine in peace and vacate the premises before the crowd arrived. Otherwise, he learned to conceal himself backstage until the others were served their snacks. Right on cue he would make a swashbuckling entrance by bursting out of the woods and flying down the slope to the garden stage like Errol Flynn in a scene from a pirate movie. He then proceeded to barge onto centre stage and help himself. Nobody ever got anything without giving up some of it to Bandit. At times he made such a hog of himself that in fun I began referring to him as Porky.

Between crowd scenes Bandit took to coming up to the

trailer and begging, an act which seemed beneath his dignity. Before my husband could empty the food container for him, Bandit would stand up in a Charlie Chaplin pose, and hold out his hands, as if to grab a chunk of food before it disappeared into a phantom's clutches. In the mornings he would come before we were up, but too old for acrobatics, he would wait outside the door for my husband and follow him à la Raggedy Ann to the shed.

Occasionally in the evening when there was a lull in the excitement Bandit would recline on the deck like a faithful watchdog. At his best he rose above the madness altogether by climbing up the arbutus tree and snoozing in the crotch of its twin trunks. Surely no king ever sat more securely in his throne than Bandit in the arbutus tree.

In her supporting role, Putzi never made a nuisance of herself, nor did she ever overstay her welcome. Her greatest delight, and here she was no exception, was eating. Unlike the others, Putzi was a connoisseur who took her time to savour her meal. In her squirrel-like squat, she would take a clump of dog food into her slim hands and, holding it to one side of her mouth, bite off a corner, then switch to the other side and repeat the ceremony before she ground up the rest. She was the least fussy of the bunch, and ate everything from dog food to left-over corn cobs to grapes to chicken bones, which were a genuine delight with the cartilage as the first and best part. She could crack open an egg with expertise, lap up the yolk, and lick the shell clean.

Having gradually overcome her reserve, Putzi had also

taken to following my husband to the shed. When he came out of the trailer, she first stood like a ballerina on a music box, then gracefully twirled on her way to the shed. This dance of hers allowed her to keep her eye on my husband and, important to her at all times, to maintain her overview of her surroundings.

By mid-summer our eccentric little Foxy had become a rare guest. All we would have needed to bring our raccoon population up to an even dozen was for Foxy to show up with three little ones of her own. Fortunately she never did, or we wouldn't have known how to manage them all.

Most people would consider one raccoon a terrible nuisance, and I could imagine the face of anyone who would have peeked over our fence to see a circus of eight or nine raccoons in our yard. As long as they got what they came for and knew exactly where they could get it, none, not even greedy Raggedy, did anything to make us regret that we had let them have the run of our place.

Over the summer the demand for dog food had risen markedly. Each time we went to the store for the next eight-kilo bag, I was expecting the cashier to ask us what kind of dog we had, or why she never saw it with us.

Our greatest challenge was not keeping our crew out of things they shouldn't get into, because we never gave them the opportunity to, but keeping them out of each other's hair. Constant traffic throughout the summer and vigorous competition escalated into turf wars and entanglements, which we tried to curtail by giving each party its own serving.

Since one group invariably finished before the other—and no one was ever satisfied as long as someone else was eating—order would erupt into chaos, dispersing raccoons in all directions and separating kits from their mothers.

After one hefty skirmish Raggedy, followed closely by Rocky, departed in a hurry, leaving baffled little Ricky to fend for himself. Since Mom and Sis had deserted him, Ricky ventured over to the big cedar log where Molly, Dolly and Bugsy were gathered around Putzi. Ricky might have done well to put himself up for adoption, but Putzi growled and snapped and would not have him.

Eventually everything calmed down. Putzi and the Racketeers went their way, and lost Ricky returned some time later in the company of his rightful family. With a greedy sister and a domineering mother who generally ignored him, poor Ricky always got the short end of the stick. He did, however, have his moment of glory when once he mustered up the courage to steal some food from Bandit, a remarkable accomplishment for a dreamy little raccoon.

Most conflicts were usually started and finished by no other than Miss Raggedy Ann. She was especially hostile towards Putzi and they once went at each other with such a vengeance that both tumbled off the garden stage and rolled onto the lawn. Despite her generally passive nature, Putzi could be aggressive when the situation demanded. Once Bandit was engaged in an altercation with Raggedy and as if to avenge herself for past grievances, Putzi sneaked up from behind and snapped at him. All in all these run-ins sounded and looked worse than they really were, and they ended in insult rather than injury.

One morning my husband actually succeeded in having all nine, including Bandit, squat and eat together on the garden stage, a feat no less than getting Canada's Premiers to sit down at the negotiating table and discuss national unity. Harmony among raccoons is as fragile as among politicians, and to avoid battle scenes on the garden stage, my husband trained Putzi and the Racketeers to feed at the other end of the yard in what used to be Foxy's spot. This worked, of course, only until one bunch finished and wandered over to see what they could grab from the other guys.

In the event of a complete break-down, we could always resort to the garden hose for crowd control. Raccoons, however, are not deterred by hoses or brooms, and after shaking themselves off in the salal, they would charge right back into action. After each fray, a wild smell lingered for some time, giving our yard the distinct odour of a raccoon ranch.

Despite the frequent fights and altercations that sometimes turned our yard into a madhouse, we continued to relish our raccoon summer. How many people have such an intense experience, and how many have the time, and appreciation, to participate in raccoon life as we could? And who knew if such an opportunity would come our way again?

Even if our raccoons continued to stick around through the year, we could hardly expect things to carry on exactly as they had. Already Putzi had started taking the Three

Racketeers on longer excursions that lasted one or two days and soon the Three Racketeers and Ricky and Rocky would strike out on their own. Their lives, and ours, were bound to change; the question was when, and how.

Top: Our home on Mayne Island.
Bottom: The garden stage.
Front cover: The one and only Miss Raggedy Ann.

Top: Putzi and the Three Racketeers.
Bottom: Dolly, Bugsy and Molly.

Top: Raggedy, Ricky and Rocky.
Bottom: Putzi and Bugsy, sole survivors.

Top: Bugsy on his own.
Bottom: The view from the top.
Back cover: Making friends with Raggedy Ann.

Chapter 6
Sickness and Sadness

One September morning my husband's sister-in-law called to inform us that a friend had seen a young emaciated raccoon with diarrhea on the property where she had been house-sitting. I could only report that we had noticed no changes in our bunch. If any of them had been suffering from diarrhea, we would most likely have never known. Not once did our raccoons leave any droppings on our property, nor did my husband ever come across any scats on his excursions up the hill.

When Putzi appeared a few weeks later with runny eyes, we were not alarmed as she'd had a similar sort of eye infection in June and had recovered quickly. This time, however, her condition spread to Molly and Dolly whose eyes became crusted with greenish matter. To our relief they developed no further symptoms that we could detect, and mother and daughters continued to eat with appetite.

On the afternoon of October the thirteenth, Putzi showed

up for the first time with only Dolly and Bugsy who played together in the trees. Independent Molly, we assumed, had gone off on her own. Putzi's eyes were showing some improvement this time although they were still crusted and tight. Dolly's eyes were in worse condition, but she seemed to experience a respite until the day after Thanksgiving, which also marked the fifth day of Molly's disappearance. Dolly's one eye was now stuck shut with green matter. Although she ate a little, she appeared weak and wobbly, and her fur lacked lustre.

Traditionally the Racketeers had always arrived and departed together but, before Putzi and Bugsy had eaten, Dolly struggled up the path and slipped through the deer fence into the woods. Like her sister, she never returned.

At first, it did not occur to us that any of our raccoons might be in any serious danger, but now with two casualties in such a short space of time we could only hope that the rest would remain robust enough to resist whatever virus was going around. Putzi's eyes had recovered to normal and lucky little Bugsy continued to stay symptom-free.

Up until this time Ricky and Rocky had been two barrels of monkeys, digging in the lawn, playing on the logs and in the trees, hiding in the salal leaves by the compost bin and getting into harmless mischief. Shortly after Dolly's disappearance, however, we noticed that Rocky was becoming tired, listless and distracted. When the twins' eyes started to run, we feared the worst.

Since Raggedy and the twins spent most of their time

around our place, we were forced to witness their rapid decline. As they sickened, Ricky and Rocky would doze or go off by themselves and hide in the cave of a decaying tree trunk below the big arbutus tree while Raggedy stood vigil or wandered back and forth in a perplexed state. Once Rocky sat on one of the plateaus in our garden and slept with her forehead butted against the ground, something we had never seen our lively young raccoons do. Despite the cute picture she made, sitting hunched over with her white-tipped ears sticking straight out like little wings, her behaviour was unsettling.

Ricky and Rocky showed little interest in their food, a lack of appetite that was totally out of character for Rocky. Both would turn their food around in their hands, put it down and wander around aimlessly on rubbery legs. I tried crunching up some dog food into smaller pieces and breaking off tiny crumbs of bread in the hope that they would take at least a nibble but their interest was minimal, and their efforts half-hearted.

My husband decided to replace the larger paddling pool with the smaller Rubbermaid container we had used earlier so that it could be cleaned more easily and regularly filled with fresh water. That Ricky and Rocky drank lots of water offered us some hope.

At the same time the twins became obsessed with cleaning themselves with an intensity we could now remember having observed in Molly and Dolly. They would sit and energetically lick their bellies, as if they were trying to relieve stomach pains. Their eyes were crusted over with sticky green matter and I don't know how they were able to get around as well as they did.

As if to comfort each other, sister and brother maintained close body contact. One day when neither Ricky and Rocky nor Raggedy showed up, my husband went into the woods to look for them and spotted little Ricky sitting with his arm around his sister. Then and there that he sensed that Rocky wasn't going to make it.

Watching Raggedy's two rapidly weaken and wither broke our hearts. Although we were expecting them to disappear as quietly as Molly and Dolly had, they kept struggling back. Early one morning we heard them cooing under the trailer and around the yard. The following morning we heard their plaintive warbling again, as if they were calling out for help.

After that Ricky and Rocky never returned. And neither did Raggedy. Except for an odd pale brown patch on her nose and some matted fur on the side of her face, she had seemed through the ordeal of losing her young so healthy and indestructible. For days we kept looking out for her and expecting our mutt to appear all of a sudden in her predictably unpredictable manner, but all in vain. It took us a long time to accept her lingering absence as definite, final, irreversible.

During all of these events our Bandit maintained his routine but after Raggedy and Ricky and Rocky disappeared, he was absent for one day. To our great relief he turned up the next afternoon, but with a matted, dishevelled coat. I was horrified to notice a green gob in the corner of his one eye when he ambled over to the trailer. I tried to tell myself that I was seeing things, that nothing was wrong with our big Bandit, but when he stumbled up the stone steps, there was little doubt that he was making his last exit.

Within two short weeks we had six casualties and since Foxy never turned up again, we had to add a seventh fatality to the list. In the meantime the *Island Tides*, a local newspaper published on Pender Island, reported an epidemic of canine distemper on Mayne Island. According to the article twenty-four raccoons had been found dead. On the basis of our numbers we assumed that the disease must have claimed a higher toll. If our casualties were representative of the island's real losses, the epidemic represented a serious setback to the local raccoon population.

Although we do not know how long our raccoons suffered on their own, their illness seemed to have progressed at a merciful speed. Had we known more about the disease, there would likely have been little we could have done to help or save our friends. We could hardly have caught them, and trying to would have caused them, and us, considerable trauma. In any case I'm not sure that we could have recruited assistance from anyone else, either considering that many people regard raccoons as nothing but pests and varmints, and are glad when they're gone.

As I read in Dorcas McClintock's *A Natural History of Raccoons*, an epizootic such as canine or feline distemper occurs naturally every so many years to act as an agent for population control and natural selection. Given the rampant nature of the disease and its place in the order of things, we had to accept Nature's last word.

When our whole yard was full of raccoons, we had wondered how things would go on; now our question had been answered. We regretted having chased Raggedy with the broom and thought that, if we had known that we would lose her, we would have let her dig up the lawn to her heart's content.

In view of the final tragedy we had to question how wise we had been to feed our raccoons in the first place. Had we not interfered with Nature when we thought we were only being kind? I don't know. Any contact between humans and wild animals, particularly when one becomes as attached to them as we were to ours, is bound to raise questions that are not so easily answered.

Admittedly we had been feeding our raccoons just as much out of self-interest as concern for their welfare. Whether our actions had been wrong or right, we had at least provided them with a safe and welcome environment in which they could rest and play. We felt neither regret nor guilt for the part we had played, and we were grateful for the memories and experiences our friends had given us.

For the longest time we mourned Bandit, Raggedy, Foxy, Molly and Dolly, Ricky and Rocky and the garden stage echoed their absence. We could hardly believe that Raggedy Ann would never put on one of her audacious performances, nor could we get used to the fact that Bandit would no longer make his cameo appearances on the big cedar log. Where once there had been activity and excitement, now there was sadness and silence.

But at least we still had Putzi and Bugsy, and their story would open with Act I, Scene I.

Chapter 7
Sole Survivors

Despite the down note on which our summer had ended with the loss of Bandit, Raggedy Ann, Ricky and Rocky, Dolly and Molly, we decided optimistically to tough out another winter on Mayne Island. To make ourselves more comfortable we bought a small space heater, and to prepare for the next inevitable power outages we snapped up a second-hand kerosene heater in August. I had also been lucky to find myself a simple second-hand word processor which would eliminate the noise I made on my rattling Thrift Store electric typewriter when both of us were confined to the trailer during a period of typical West Coast winter rain.

After one year on Mayne Island we had made progress in our ability to live simply and within our means. Our expenses, including property taxes, utilities, and car repairs, averaged out at $840 a month with a low of $503 and a high of $1471. On top of basic living expenses, we had spent a total of

$1820 on improvements to the trailer and yard. Although we could always imagine further upgrades, we did not foresee any major budget-straining investments. In all we could say: so far, so good.

Even at the low end of our budget we were not living badly, and we didn't lack or deny ourselves anything we considered essential. We did not live on steak and champagne, but we never had, and we didn't need to, either. Our wholesome diet combined vegetarian and lighter meat dishes, all home-made.

A new grocery store had opened up at the Mayne Street Mall that spring so we were able to do the bulk of our shopping locally. As a result our trips to Salt Spring Island were less hectic and laden, and ended up being a welcome diversion to our reclusive life on Mayne.

The major challenge in our simple lifestyle turned out to be neither living with financial nor spatial limitations, but withstanding what I call one's dark moments, particularly when the Pineapple Express drove rain at us sideways, the windows fogged up with condensation, the roof came down on our heads, and we started to think that we may have made the biggest mistake of our lives.

What we had undertaken may appear romantic and thrilling at first; which is exactly how the idea seemed when we first discussed quitting our jobs and returning to Canada. Surely there are those of you out there, particularly many restless Baby Boomers, whose deepest desire has always been to leave the rat race behind, take for the highway like Sal

Paradise and go in search of the life-altering lessons the road has in store for us, if we're open to them. (Does the familiar voice tempt and seduce? Do you feel a hook and a line pulling at your insides? Are the ants in your pants getting up to dance?) Well, I can say that I had first dreamed of doing exactly what we were doing as early as the age of sixteen, and here I was twenty-seven years later.

Before you hand in that letter of resignation or put your house up for sale, let me first offer a word of caution! Most of us are not aware of the firmness of the framework in which we grow up and live until we step outside of it. We never realize how much of our life is determined by someone or something outside of ourselves—our parents, our teachers, our friends, our superiors and bosses, our clients and customers—until none of them is around to tell us what to do, and when, why, and how to do it!

Unless you are self-driven and self-directed, you will find that the journey on the less trodden path is not all sunshine and roses. With excess time on your hands and no job to shape your days, no shopping mall or coffee shop or fitness studio around the corner, most of you will end up packing it in after a few months because a. you don't know what to do with yourselves anymore, and b. as a couple that now spends all their time together you will start getting on each other's nerves.

Fortunately we've never been consumer junkies and we do not derive our self-esteem from what we own or can present to others. We also happen to be fiercely independent people who can always amuse and occupy ourselves. I had my writing projects, and my husband liked to work around outside. Used to each other's company and conversation we have always been able to resolve our differences without letting them deteriorate into resentments or pile up into major conflicts.

Our greatest difficulties turned out not to be with each other; rather each with him/herself. Every now and then we went through a phase of self-criticism, doubt or worry, which any psychologist worth her degree will confirm is natural when one goes through a dramatic change in one's life. These downs were exacerbated by periods of nasty weather, but luckily these moments were as temporary as they were normal. Soon enough the rain would let up, and the sun would come out so that we could go for a walk. And believe me, there's nothing more helpful than a walk to dispel a bout of depression or self-pity, and there was no better therapy to boost our spirits than a visit from Putzi and Bugsy!

Although Putzi had recovered from distemper and Bugsy had been blessed with good genes, we worried that our two survivors might not be out of the woods just yet. One afternoon Bugsy fell asleep with his head down against the ground, a position which reminded me so much of Rocky when she was sick that I became alarmed. Eventually he got up and went off with his mother. And I was never so glad to see him go!

Throughout the fall, Putzi and Bugsy were as inseparable as Siamese twins. In the morning they usually arrived shortly before we got up and when I opened the curtain we would often see them sitting side by side and shoulder to shoulder.

We abandoned the garden stage for logistical as well as sentimental reasons, and continued to feed our sole survivors at the opposite end of the yard next to our trailer. This location offered us the opportunity to observe our two furry friends from our bedroom window every morning and afternoon. It also allowed mother and son to enter or exit the yard by slipping through the deer fence or by following a steep natural trail from the upper woods down a rocky, treed slope to the flat landing at the top of three stone steps. Here they could dine or hang around without disturbance.

Since my husband would get up and feed Putzi and Bugsy first thing in the morning, I would sit or kneel at the window and watch them as they monitored his activity inside the trailer with the keenest attention. When my husband zipped up his jacket and turned the door knob, their ears would prick up and their heads turn. As soon as he stepped outside, they would wiggle their behinds and slowly back up in anticipation.

Usually we kept a dish of food in the trailer, but if my husband had to go to the shed to fill up, Putzi and Bugsy would first hesitate, then at Putzi's lead, bound down the steps and gallop over the grass like Butch Cassidy and the Sundance Kid running from the law. Since they tended to take a roundabout route on their way back or get caught up under the trailer, my husband sometimes had to wait for them. "C'mon, c'mon," he'd say to them and they would hop up the steps and wriggle and wiggle as he threw their food on the ground.

Bugsy was a real meat and potatoes man and preferred his dog food to anything else. Putzi turned up her nose at nothing and liked to start with a heel of whole wheat bread, which she could grab and retreat with to a large flat rock where she enjoyed her starter in privacy. While Bugsy was unconcerned and blissful unless his mother made a sudden move, Putzi was constantly on the watch for danger and there was very little that escaped her finely tuned receiver.

Occasionally they squabbled and growled at each other, particularly when they got down to the last few pieces of food. By and large they remained on amicable terms and never staged the kind of riotous scenes that had gone on in the summer. Numbers, it would seem, bring out the worst in animals, just as crowds do in humans.

Curious as to how and when our devoted pair would part ways, we began to anticipate changes in their routine and habits. When they were having communication problems, Bugsy would perch strategically forward on the clearing above the top step while Putzi sat behind him. We understood the few times that Bugsy appeared first or alone to signal the big break-up, but back they'd come, together again, until the next falling out, and so they continued into December.

As winter set in, Putzi and Bugsy began coming only once a day and usually after dark so that the best we got to see of them were shadowy shapes. During periods of unpleasant weather, they would miss a day or two but, more often than not, they'd put on their fur coats and go out for their favourite snack. With no intruders to compete with anymore, Putzi and Bugsy remained faithful customers, and our sole survivors helped us get through some of our darker winter moments.

Three days before Christmas it snowed at night, with flurries continuing during the day. On the night of the twenty-third another twenty centimetres fell. We were running low on groceries, and since our van didn't have snow tires, we decided we'd better trudge the two kilometres over to the village and get as many supplies as we could comfortably carry back. By Christmas Eve Day the snow had accumulated to thirty centimetres, which for the Gulf Islands was a significant amount, ten centimetres being a major snowfall when the Coast often receives no more than a dusting at a time.

Christmas Day was the kind of brilliant, tranquil winter day one sees pictured on calendars. On the twenty-seventh the scene changed when snow fell relentlessly. As we watched, we couldn't help but wonder when the snowfall was ever going to let up. When we turned on the t.v., we saw that weather warnings had been issued for the entire South Coast. The Pineapple Express was due to collide with Arctic outflow winds travelling through the Fraser Valley, and Environment Canada was predicting as much as fifty centimetres of snow.

On December the twenty-eighth the worst blizzard in seventy-five years unloaded an unprecedented eighty centimetres of snow on the Gulf Islands and shut down the city of Victoria, which had received one hundred and twenty-four centimetres in twenty-four hours. The year was ending, it seemed thanks to the Wicked Witch of the North, in the Storm of the Century.

By the time the storm abated, our yard was a mountain of snow. Grossly distorted outlines were all we could recognize of any landmark in the yard, and the roofs of our trailer, shed and van bore thick burdens. After managing to unstick the frozen trailer door and to clear away the snow from the doorstep with a small frying pan (like many islanders we did not own a snow shovel), my husband laboured at digging out hip-deep walkways in the yard with the garden spade in order to get the frantic juncos and varied thrushes fed before the snow covered everything up again. Had any more snow fallen, he would not have known where to put it.

For anyone with a vivid imagination and an ability to take the circumstances lightly, the scene was as enchanting as any straight out of a fairy tale. The surrounding trees had been festively decorated since Christmas with heavy formations of snow that resembled angels' wings. I guess a pair of these must have belonged to the competent guardian who got us through the ordeal safely! Our cedar hedge had been transformed into a hooded choir that bent and leaned under the weight of their gowns. The two potted azaleas in the garden wore thick bonnets and as the temperatures rose, rocks in the yard emerged, sporting white wigs in the style of Mozart. All around clumps of snow crashed down from high branches, leaving dimples in the blanket below and sending bursts of powder into the air like feathers from a pillow fight.

In the yard there was always a banquet of birds pecking at any feed they could find, and we were glad that we managed to feed as many of them as we did. Many deer, particularly young ones like the loner that had been coming around lately without its mother, had probably not survived. We could only hope that Putzi and Bugsy had found themselves a cozy refuge where they could hole up and weather the storm.

The blizzard and its aftermath were something neither of us had ever experienced—and I lived the first twenty-seven years of my life in Saskatchewan! Although we, along with everyone else, had not reckoned on a major blizzard, we had had the foresight, or just plain luck perhaps, to stock up on kerosene for our emergency heater. We still had supplies from our last trip to Salt Spring, but the fresh groceries we had bought on our walk into the village would just last us to the end of the week.

On the twenty-ninth it was still snowing but temperatures were rising and the forecast was for freezing rain, which would put additional strain on roofs and other structures that were not built to withstand the extra weight. Promptly on New Year's morning, the power went out. All we could do was pray that it would come back on before we ran out of fuel. The snow was piled solidly up against our gate, and it wasn't until a week after the storm that we were finally able to make it out of our yard.

Our New Year's celebration that year was the most sober one ever. Cheer came not out of a bottle of champagne, this being the first time we had ever rung in a dry New Year, but from the sight the following morning of Bugsy, our Crown Prince, perched on a big tree stump next to the tall fir tree that guarded the raccoon's feeding spot. I stepped outside to give him some food, but I had no way of reaching his accustomed spot without getting stuck in snow up to my waist. My husband had managed to clear only the necessary trail to the outhouse so the only place I could scatter food was on the step outside the door.

At first Bugsy hesitated. He seemed, despite his hunger, unable to get it through his head that the food on the step was his if only he would come and get it. He did finally manage to overcome himself and wade through the snow down to the back of the trailer, but immediately he turned around and climbed back up again. Like Humpty–dumpty he sat for a while on the stump before foregoing his treat and exiting through the deer fence.

Shortly after midnight on New Year's Day the power came back on. By the end of the following week the snow had melted and the islands had recovered from the shock. The Storm of the Century had heightened our awareness of how much we take for granted in our modern world, and of how helpless we can seem when Nature causes man–made conveniences to fail and cuts us down to size.

Those situations in which one finds oneself at the mercy of powers beyond one's control can act like strong medicine, which despite its bitter taste swiftly cures any delusions one might entertain about man's ability to outsmart Nature. The storm made us mindful of Nature's predominance and of our own insignificance in the natural world. The calm that followed gave us occasion to reflect upon the lessons in humility and gratitude our simple life had taught us, and to value well-being and peace of mind as our prize possessions.

We considered ourselves fortunate to have come out of the Storm of the Century without any damage to our trailer or our property. What we hoped for next was a stretch of good weather and the return of Putzi and Bugsy. And the sooner they turned up, the better.

Chapter 8
Changes

With the worst of a record-breaking winter behind us, we longed for signs of spring. In late February the quadraphonic performance of the tree frogs started up, and courting combat could be heard in the woods from evening into late night. Judging by the decrease in intensity and frequency of scuffles in our vicinity over last year, we didn't need an exact body count to confirm how seriously the distemper outbreak had decimated the raccoon population in the fall. Since mating activity took place at night, we could never tell how many were carrying on in our yard at a time.

Putzi and Bugsy continued to show up, but only after it was already dark. Bugsy did not seem yet mature enough to assume Bandit's role. Whereas females are ready to breed at ten to twelve months, males are not sexually mature until two years. Unless Bugsy was really a Babsie and a qualified suitor for Putzi made his claim to the territory soon, our family expectations for the summer would have to remain pessimistic.

One February afternoon my husband was up in our woods where he spotted Putzi and Bugsy in one tree and a third raccoon in another. A couple of weeks later a stranger began sneaking up to the deer fence from the neighbouring property. Another evening while we were outside watching Putzi and Bugsy have their snack, the newcomer approached and stood up on the flat rock where Putzi liked to enjoy a private moment with a heel of bread. Guarding their supper like vultures, Putzi and Bugsy first growled, then when the customary intimidation tactics failed, Putzi chased the intruder off.

Number Three, as we first called it, made itself scarce until April when it worked up the nerve to check our place out again. A size bigger than Bugsy and probably a year older, Number Three made appearances that were interspersed with long absences. On account of its roundish ears that were slightly flattened like a teddy bear's, we named it Teddy. From its shy, excitable and submissive nature we assumed that Teddy was a female.

By studying each animal's particular habits and mannerisms, we had learned with remarkable accuracy to distinguish one raccoon from the other, and male from female as well. Of course a peek under Teddy's tail would have been more scientific, but not even Raggedy would have let one of us get that close!

Being more agreeable than his mother, Bugsy let Teddy join him. Whereas Bugsy accepted her unconditionally, Putzi took violent exception. In early June after numerous threats and rejections, Teddy was finally suffered at the dinner table, albeit with Putzi's disdain, and she became our first new addition to the extended family.

Bugsy's frequent solo appearances seemed to indicate a developing independent streak, but Putzi's growing hostility left no doubt that as far as she was concerned it was high time that Bugsy struck out on his own. Their late spring routine brought them into our yard frequently before we got up, and sometimes their disagreements woke us. One morning I lifted the curtain to find them sitting some distance apart. Bugsy tried to approach Putzi, but she growled and lunged and drove him off. When I looked out the window later, he was standing behind her with his arms draped over her haunches. Putzi did not in any way appreciate Bugsy's attempts to discover his manhood, if that was what he was doing, and she promptly retreated to her favourite flat rock where she kept a frosty distance.

When Bugsy wandered through on his own during the very early morning, we would awaken to overturned plants, scattered clumps of moss and general disorder in my husband's rock garden. Although we had not caught him in the act, we suspected that Bugsy had come looking for snacks at night and in his adolescent restlessness had started digging around the plants.

Familiar with raccoon determination in the person of the late Miss Raggedy Ann, we had already learned that the best method of dealing with a raccoon's bad behaviour was to change our own ways. My husband therefore decided to salvage his rock garden by moving most of the plants to a location near the shed. He knew of course that there would be no guarantee that they would be left alone in another place, but as it turned out, Bugsy was only going through another phase.

With brief interruptions, Putzi and Bugsy would drop in together sometime between supper and bedtime. Whenever I watched them from our window, I couldn't help but imagine them dressed up in tuxedos, white shirts with bow ties and shiny top hats, and swinging canes in their gloved hands as they entertained us like a Vaudeville duo. Often we stayed up past our bedtime, just so we wouldn't miss them.

One Sunday night we were watching t.v. when we heard a soft scratching or brushing noise on the trailer door. We didn't give the matter much thought and after eleven o'clock we turned off the t.v. and started to get ready for bed. It was a lovely warm night, so my husband went outside to take a look at the stars. Well, there were Putzi and Bugsy sitting outside like Trick-or-treaters, who lacked the gumption to knock again. At times like these I thought how handy it would be to have a loaded video surveillance camera above our door.

As well as enjoying such late night surprise visits, we got the greatest kick out of watching our twosome drink from the pail of water we kept next to the trailer. The more experimental of the pair, young Bugsy climbed over the rock garden and down the rock wall to position himself headfirst over the pail while Putzi tended to choose the conventional route down the steps and along the ground. Using a rock as a foot stool and showing an elegant ankle, she would reach for the rim of the pail and hang on while she drank.

To test their reactions, we called out to them. Most of the time they would turn and look up and later, knowing that we were still watching at the window, they would lift their heads voluntarily. Once in a while they descended in tandem and stuck their heads into the pail. At moments like this we could not imagine Mother and Son ever splitting up.

Into spring the bond between Putzi and Bugsy started showing signs of wear and tear. In the morning we could hear them scrapping outside our trailer or fighting in the woods at night. We were not sure what to expect from their on-again off-again relationship, and we often thought they had separated when in fact they hadn't. Their story may not have been as suspenseful as a murder mystery, but for us it was certainly as enthralling.

On Good Friday morning Putzi and Bugsy got into another early scrap but took off before we got up. In the afternoon they returned for a drink. We had left out some chicken bones which Putzi proceeded to clean up while Bugsy climbed a tree on our neighbour's side of the deer fence and began cooing. During times of stress he reverted to behaviour more reminiscent of a baby raccoon than a yearling. Putzi, of course, was not going to fall for any childish nonsense and while she devoted her full attention to her chicken bones, Bugsy cooed himself out.

The next day Putzi appeared without Bugsy, who did not

turn up until a week later in the early morning. Since we hadn't left out any extra food in the evening, Bugsy proceeded to dig around in what was left of the rock garden. Not finding anything as satisfying as crunchy, he sat huddled up on a rock like a homeless waif while Putzi, who arrived a little later, maintained her distance. It was still too early for us to hop out of bed. As fond as we were of them, we did draw the line!

At last they left, but that night they returned for supper. After a week of independence, Bugsy had apparently come back home to Mommy with his dirty laundry and a hearty appetite. And so they continued, the best of friends, until the middle of June.

Yelping and whimpering noises in the night indicated that Putzi and Bugsy were going through another crisis. Early one morning we awoke to discover Putzi growling, snapping and lunging at Bugsy in earnest. After a half-hearted effort to growl back, Bugsy retreated to higher ground where he cowered next to a tree. He risked a few steps toward Putzi, but this time she did not back down as she had done in the past. Our last look out of the window before we got up revealed Bugsy cringing on a rock and staring into our bedroom window while Putzi resolutely ignored him.

For the first time mother and son did not breakfast together. In fact after my husband had dished out their food, Bugsy remained down by the trailer and did not dare to approach Putzi while she ate. My husband put Bugsy's breakfast on the top of the big flat boulder next to our trailer on the same spot where Bandit had occasionally eaten. Of course when Putzi saw the special attention Bugsy was getting, she stood up to her full height to see what he had that she didn't, but she stayed on her side. Bugsy finished his breakfast, then wandered up to the top of the yard and after a brief glance, off he went.

Officially on his own from that day on, Bugsy remained in tune with Putzi's rhythms, and he'd turn up either shortly before or after his mother. Once separation had taken place, Putzi would not tolerate Bugsy. With the exception of one moment of either maternal weakness or temporary indifference when she stooped to share her food with him, she made every attempt to drive him away until he moved automatically to his newly designated table a couple of yards away.

Teddy on the other hand was tolerated most of the time. Her attitude was generally submissive and cautious, and rightly so, especially after an incident in which Putzi poked Teddy repeatedly in the rear end with her nose until she moved off. Putzi's generosity depended upon her mood, which was more often than not a cantankerous one. When we recalled last summer's struggles, we would not have expected our passive Putzi to turn into the ferocious matriarch who now took charge.

Putzi's dominance, however, did not assure her exclusive rights to our place. In summer Bugsy and Teddy would often be around at the same time and since my husband fed them at two different places, they would wander over after a drink to check out the size of Putzi's serving or to clean up her left-overs. Summer rehearsals, by the looks of things, had begun.

In the meantime Bugsy and Teddy had become a real item. It seemed that Bugsy, our good-natured little innocent, was either too used to company to go it alone, or else he had been severely bitten by the lovebug. For awhile Bugsy and Teddy often travelled together. One night while Putzi went down to the pail for a drink, Bugsy and Teddy made a bee-line for the pile of food she'd left unattended. On their way they must have had second thoughts, because they stopped instead to groom and nuzzle each other. We had seen them before briefly licking or touching noses. This time we were able to watch them actually kiss and cuddle like a pair of young lovers.

By July Bugsy had gained in weight and size, and his ratty tail filled out to a bushy full-sized baton. Eventually his adolescent infatuation with Teddy passed, and he took up the life of a loner. No matter how long he went off on his own, Bugsy always knew where to find home, and crunchy. Although he was not tame enough to eat out of our hands like Raggedy Ann had been, he accepted our presence as if we were native plants growing in the yard. Despite the hard lessons he must have been learning out there in the wild woods, he remained such a good-natured pushover that we had a hard time imagining him ever taking over Big Daddy Bandit's role.

From our furry friends we had learned two things: that

apart from hunger and death, change is all one can be reasonably sure of in life, and that when change comes it asks neither our permission nor our approval. In the mid-90's, a building boom was taking place on the West Coast and with it came an increase in construction activity on the Gulf Islands.

Of course, when one lives in a wet climate, which in 1997 beginning with the Storm of the Century was producing some of the wettest and most miserable weather conditions in recorded meteorological history, one takes advantage of every dry day to build and repair. Although noise by-laws exist on the Gulf Islands, they are not as easily or strictly enforced as they are in urban areas. On the smaller islands there is not the administrative personnel or full-time police presence to handle complaints, and the island mentality tends to be more non-conformist and even laissez-faire.

As secluded as we felt behind our gate, we were not immune to the accelerating impact development was having on island life, particularly, when hammering in the neighbourhood went on well into the evening and over the weekend. One summer afternoon out of an impulse to vent some of my exasperation I wrote a song, which I titled *Summer on the Islands:*

D.S. Hartley

In winter it rains; you go almost insane
When the sky's a horse blanket of grey.
So, unless you go south to Mexico,
You can't wait for spring's first balmy ray.
Like the rush of the tide, we all head outside;
In the garden there's so much to do.
After all the work's done,
Summertime's meant for fun—
Boy, have I got some big news for you!

Summer on the islands,
Where living's as sweet as a peach.
Chainsaws are goin', folks are out mowin',
And it's party time on the beach!
Summer on the islands,
It's B.C. at its best!
There's so much commotion
The roar drowns out the ocean.
How's a person to get any rest?

No spot under the sun should rate Number One
On the list of God's Top Ten Creations
Like the Southern Gulf Isles--you can travel for miles
To find beauty like this in our nation.
I can't help but see when they leave the ferry,
Why tourists fall madly in love
With the beaches, the sea, the mountains, the trees—
Here's Paradise they've always dreamed of!

Oh, summer on the islands,
It's as quiet as a mouse
'Til the next urban dreamer
Moves spouse, kids, dog, Beemer
And starts building another house.
Yes, summer on the islands,
It's as peaceful as can be.
The singing of birds can hardly be heard
For the crash of a falling tree!

True peace and quiet, you're hard pressed to find it
When a boom's underway in construction.
Progress these days moves in very strange ways
That resemble the eve of destruction.
Rather than blessed, I often feel stressed
Each time there's a new building project.
Will we ever get enough of this development stuff
Before nothing's left to preserve or protect?

Summer on the islands,
In the evening it's lovely and cool.
Dammit, here come the boys,
Making all kinds of noise
With their blasted power tools!
Summer on the islands
Could be Heaven without a doubt
If not for buzz, wham and clang,
Boom, zzzz, thud and bang.
God, please make the power go out!

No, I won't get upset; the world's not ending yet.
The craziness will surely wind down.
After Labour Day, I guess, the noise will be less
When at last all the crowds head for town.
Then I'll go take a look, find a great big fat book
To curl up with some fine starry eve.
I sure will be glad, winter's not all that bad:
It's an islander's soothing reprieve.

Oh, winter on the islands,
Can life anywhere be this good?
Let's drink a toast now, my dear,--
Hey, what's that I hear?
It's the neighbour and he's outside chopping wood!

Part of me was just having fun with the idea of progress in Paradise, but most of me was feeling downright frustrated by disturbances in the immediate neighbourhood. We may have been more sensitive to noise than most locals, but as lovers of tranquillity we weren't a complete anomaly. Similar resentments to ours appeared in *The Driftwood*, published on Salt Spring Island, in the form of a raging debate over how the Southern Gulf Islands should handle present and future development, and at the same time "preserve and protect" their uniqueness, one of the principle mandates upon which the Islands Trust was set up.

At risk was the hallowed island way of life that many people had moved and retired to the Gulf Islands to enjoy. At issue were concerns about land use and the environment, the supply and quality of drinking water, logging practises, endangered plant and wildlife, economic and commercial development, to name a few. As more and more people moved onto the islands and carted their urban standards and city expectations over with them, the traditional islander and the unconventional country recluse were soon going to be as endangered as many native plants and wildlife.

Important questions had arisen to which we had to find answers. Could we continue to live the kind of life that had tempted us to give up our jobs and move to Mayne Island in the first place, and if so for how long? Was there anything we could do ourselves to adjust better to the situation around us, and how effective would our efforts be? Or did we need a change altogether? Should we emerge from our shell and go somewhere else that had perhaps more to offer socially and economically? As much as we liked our property, we were not so attached to it that we couldn't conceive of ever leaving. We still preferred the West Coast as a location, but knew there were other places and islands that were just as attractive as Mayne Island.

In order to come up with a final solution we would need to give ourselves some time to let our thoughts settle and for answers to come by themselves, which experience has shown us often helps determine the course of one's life in difficult times. We would have, however, to make the first move. At the end of May we decided to put our property up for sale.

Chapter 9
Full Circle

From a purely practical point of view we could not envision living indefinitely in a travel trailer. So far we had put more energy than funds into improvements, and we had succeeded with modest means in making our yard attractive, and our small living space homey. We had also become good at managing problems such as condensation inside the trailer and at dodging overhanging cupboards that could be a hazard if my husband, who is tall, stood up suddenly without paying attention and banged his head. To make our place more liveable over the long term, however, we would need to invest more money which, given the building restrictions on the property, did not make a lot of sense.

Rather than involve a real estate agent, we decided to try and sell our place ourselves. Given the property's limitations, we did not expect to attract just any buyer; in fact we had no idea what kind of response we'd get, if at all, from the ad we placed in the *Island Tides*.

In the event that we could neither sell nor get the price we were asking, we were prepared in the meantime to check out other possibilities. A neighbour down the road showed us the one-hundred-square-foot mini-cabin he'd built on his property. We could see that if one was skilled, ingenious and resourceful one could make a very small structure quite attractive and comfortable.

Another solution would be to move the Silver Streak out and drive a bigger RV in, since all that was required to get around the covenant, as we understood from discussions we'd had on the issue with acquaintances from the neighbourhood, was that the "dwelling" not be fixed to the ground or to a foundation. There were choices, but before we went ahead and got excited about plans and projects, we wanted first to give selling a go.

If our future on Mayne Island was uncertain for the time being, there was one thing, however, that we could rely on, and that was the continued company of our raccoons. With no major competition to fend off and Bugsy out of her hair at last, Putzi did not hesitate to take full advantage of her independence. Free to come and go as she pleased, she roamed the grounds as if she owned them, and we came to think of our place as Putzi's place.

Putzi's casual routine suggested that our Queen of the House was going to have a summer vacation from the rigours of motherhood. Putzi often arrived well before we were up. Sometimes she stared patiently at the trailer window for signs of movement within, or she used the opportunity to catch up on the sleep she must have lost during the summer months she'd spent raising the Racketeers. After she'd finished eating in the evening she frequently hung around for a digestive pause. Like a pet she'd stretch out and lay her head on a pillow-sized patch of grass. Given the invitation, she would have crawled right into bed with us.

When she wasn't relaxing, Putzi would stick out one slim black hind leg like a figure in a Toulouse-Lautrec poster, and clean herself. Sometimes she came around just for the exercise and climbed one of the tall fir trees in our yard. It was not unusual for her to pass through for a refreshment from the pail of water next to the trailer. Once after she'd had a big morning drink, she climbed a tree. About an hour later we went outside to find her curled up like a furry nest on a high branch. I don't know how she managed to sleep up there without falling off, but then it just goes to show how effortlessly raccoons can master peril!

Throughout the summer Putzi was on patrol. We were never sure exactly when to expect her and found ourselves often waiting for her like loyal servants. She was the most appreciative guest, and her strategy for getting seconds was not to beg or pester like Raggedy Ann had done, but to sit and wait.

The only time our best girl ever appeared to have got into some mischief was when she showed up once with sticky dirty hands the size and shape of baseball gloves. She had been digging around somewhere, and had likely been into some kind of insect nest. Despite the handicap she managed to pick up the dry dog food and, after making it up a tree, she came back down awhile later ready to go out on the town with perfectly manicured hands.

That summer Putzi defended her privacy with a vehemence that reminded us of Bandit, last summer's departed Daddy. Although she was doing an impressive job of running the show, we expected that sooner or later a male usurper, be it a stranger or an assertive Bugsy, would take over the territory and upset the order.

In the second week of July a fourth raccoon made its appearance in the evening. The next time it showed up after we'd had supper and it sat long enough next to the deer fence for us to guess this one to be a young female. The silvery blond tones in her long, wavy fur and the dark shawl-like patch draped across one shoulder made me picture a star of the Silver Screen, and we named her Silver.

Silver frightened easily, so my husband had to gingerly toss her a few pieces of dog food at a time until she learned that he was no threat. For the longest time she would retreat into the neighbouring yard and grip the wire fence in both hands until my husband backed away from the food pile. Although Silver ran away at first, she rarely fled farther than one of the trees on the other side of the deer fence where she consumed a chunk before sneaking down to grab the next handful. She gave us glimpses of her charm in the way she stood up behind a tree on the other side of the fence and played Peekaboo with us. We wondered if from her coyness she didn't possess some of the wiles that had so endeared

Raggedy Ann to us.

Our raccoons' routine varied without notice. Into July Silver began appearing irregularly. Her stays were short, but once in awhile she would allow herself a brief rest on a comfortable rock. Although we could see no evidence under all that beautiful fur that she was lactating, I suspected from her attentiveness and readiness to flee that she must have babies close at hand.

Putzi continued to maintain her dominance and she took every opportunity to be cantankerous towards Bugsy and Teddy, who were always more interested in eating than fighting. Once separation had taken place, Putzi would absolutely not tolerate Bugsy. Teddy, on the other hand, was frequently endured. Teddy's attitude was wary, and rightly so, after the way Putzi would lunge at her and use her nose as a poker. Although Silver managed to avoid Putzi and the others by coming in the late afternoon, their paths occasionally crossed, resulting in the usual raccoon run-ins.

One Sunday in late June our first major skirmish with all four raccoons in the yard foreshadowed the return of last summer's program. Of course, without babies yet to complicate matters, there was not the same crazed activity or competition that had characterised last summer. Frequent excitement in the woods at night assured us, however, that the situation would soon escalate.

With all the new activity we were pleased and proud that our faery garden was once again a menagerie cum sanctuary. Besides Putzi and Bugsy, and now Teddy and Silver, there was

Winston and Glorietta, our resident robin pair, and Bobby and B.J., our rufous-sided towhee couple, among other creatures, both single and attached. Should there be the threat of a Great Flood, the first seats on our Ark had already been reserved, and there were still plenty left to accommodate some little passengers as well.

At the end of July my husband heard familiar cooing outside the trailer and woke me up in the early morning. Dawn had not quite broken, but we could make out a larger raccoon we assumed to be Silver in the company of four babies. From their size they were probably a few weeks older than the Racketeers had been on their first visit.

The little acrobats were crawling, climbing, tumbling, and snooping all over the place as they checked out the water pail three at a time, tipped over flower pots or squatted in them with their furry rears hanging over the edge while they explored and dug around. A series of tracks leading from the muddy mess in the water pail over our deck to our garden chairs and table provided plenty of clues as to what they were up to after we'd gone back to sleep. The little rascals had left practically nothing untouched or unturned, and we were elated!

The second time Silver's family came in the evening. When my husband went out to feed them, they all scattered up the hill and into the trees, reassembling only after it got dark. Once Silver was accompanied by only one baby, a small male I assumed like Bugsy used to be. The other times she came with only a couple of babies that we could catch sight of in the dusk. When they encountered Putzi, the entire family dispersed.

The advent of Polly, Sal, Rosemary and Tim, the Scarborough Four as I named them, not only brought our numbers back up to last summer's count, but the new babies replaced the four we had lost. Nature couldn't have shown us more plainly and more delightfully her ability to recover her losses.

Silver kept her family under guard and brought them only three or four times late at night. I suppose it was just as well that we never got as close to the Scarborough Four as we had to Bugsy's sisters, Dolly and Molly, and Raggedy's Ricky and Rocky, or it would have been that much harder for us to accept the offer we received from a young woman who'd grown up on the island. She had first shown interest in our place shortly after we had advertised it, but like most of the inquirers she didn't call or come back.

Towards the end of August we had almost given up on finding a committed buyer and were not going to renew our ad when the young woman called to say that she was still interested. She came by and my husband set up a time the next morning to take her up to the top of the property.

The next morning Putzi made an early appearance at six-thirty. In no great hurry to leave after she had eaten, she relaxed in a couple of her favourite places, or slept. After two and a half hours she was still hanging around when V. arrived. Instead of running off at the sound and sight of a stranger, Putzi came down from her comfortable spot to drink out of the water pail in full view. We wondered if Putzi hadn't already sensed that something was afoot. Her presence seemed to indicate that the place was *her* place, and that whoever moved onto it would have to respect her right of residency.

My husband took V. up to the top of the talus slope, and later that afternoon she returned with a written offer which we took another day to talk over. The next day we met again, and made a counter offer, which V. accepted. The deal was signed and the new owner would take possession in a week.

It didn't take us long to organize our possessions, load them into our van and get ready to go on a trip to visit family and friends in Saskatchewan. We've always found that a long trip allows us to gain distance, especially when there are emotional attachments to the place we are leaving, and the time we spend on the road builds enthusiasm for the next step, particularly when the details are not yet clear. (By the time we returned to the Coast in September, we were ready to move on to Salt Spring Island, where we had first started out together.)

With gratitude for the experiences we had gathered and for the raccoon friends we had made on our little slice of Mayne Island, we left at the end of August the place that had been our simple home for two years. The garden stage was deserted, but memory summoned the entire cast as if for one last curtain call. All our friends were present in spirit: Bandit, Foxy, Raggedy Ann, Ricky and Rocky, Molly and Dolly, Putzi and Bugsy, Teddy, Silver and the Scarborough Four, whose last appearance had made a perfect going-away present.

In the crotch of the arbutus tree we could still see Bandit sleeping like a king and, of course, the tempestuous Raggedy Ann tailed us to the gate. Before he closed the gate behind him, my husband scattered one last feast in the woods next to the trailer for our friends when they came. And come they would. They would come and go, and come and go again, ever free and wild, forever true to their nature.

Appendix
The Southern Gulf Islands

The Southern Gulf Islands form a picturesque archipelago of thirteen islands and islets which lie in the Strait of Georgia off the West Coast of British Columbia between Vancouver and Vancouver Island. Salt Spring, Galiano, North and South Pender, Mayne and Saturna are the largest and all five are populated. Because of their location on the Pacific, their mild climate, luxuriant natural beauty and the absence of industry, these islands could also be called Canada's Paradise Islands.

The Gulf Islands were first discovered in the 1700's by the Spanish explorer, Juan de Fuca. As Europeans and Asians moved onto the islands in the mid-1800's, communities were established around agricultural, logging and fishing activities. In the early 1900's tourism began to play an economic role, eventually leading in the 1970's to a constant influx of weekenders and holidayers that has not subsided to this day. The rural charm of the islands presents an idyllic setting for people to turn off and get away from the hectic of the city, and their unique natural environment and laid-back atmosphere continue to make the Gulf Islands the home of choice for pensioners, weekenders, environmentalists, artists, musicians, writers, craftspeople and of course those dreamers and recluses who wish to try out alternative lifestyles.

To access Galiano, Mayne, Pender and Salt Spring from

the mainland travellers must take the Gulf Islands ferry, which sails twice a day from Tswassen on the mainland along one of the most scenic and leisurely routes on the West Coast. From Vancouver Island smaller ferries sail to Mayne, Galiano and Pender. To reach Saturna, the most outlying and remote island, one must transfer at Village Bay on Mayne, which was chosen because of its central location among the islands as a transfer hub. Salt Spring Island, the largest and most developed island, has two regular ferry connections to Vancouver Island at Fulford Harbour and Vesuvius.

Although ferry travel is a necessary part of the island way-of-life, native islanders enjoy a kind of love-hate relationship with BC Ferries which not only transports people and goods, but provides a considerable number of islanders with a steady income.

The Gulf Islands are administered by the Islands Trust, a body of twenty-six elected representatives from the thirteen most populated islands, including the Northern Gulf Islands. The Islands Trust was created by a legislative act largely to preserve the unique nature and environment of the area and to protect the islands from destruction and development.

Mayne Island

Measuring twenty-one square kilometres, Mayne Island is the smallest of the five major islands and has a year-round population of about nine hundred. As on all the islands, the population explodes during the summer months when temporary residents come to their cottages and summer houses for the holidays, and numerous tourists stay at the various Bed & Breakfasts, resorts and inns. Among Mayne's permanent residents are farmers, ferry workers, tradespeople, retirees, artists, writers and musicians, and small business people who earn their living primarily from tourism.

The "village", as all the islands' commercial centres tend ambitiously to be known, is located at Miners Bay, which was named after the gold miners who stopped over in the late 1850's on their way from Victoria to the Fraser River and the Cariboo. During the island's early settlement, ships loading and unloading passengers, mail and freight made regular calls at the wharf at Miners Bay, and Mayne Island became the Gulf Islands' first commercial and social centre.

Miners Bay is where most of the island's businesses and services are located. Local theatre productions and concerts, art shows, antique sales, meetings and various social and cultural events take place at the Agricultural Hall, affectionately shortened to Ag Hall.

The Springwater Lodge, just a short stroll from the Trading Post, is the oldest continuously-operating hotel in

British Columbia and an ideal spot from which to watch the sun set over Miners Bay and to enjoy a glass of B.C. wine or a pint of local beer.

Mayne's most notorious historical site is the Plumper Pass Lock-up, until 1900 the only jail on the Gulf Islands and now a museum. Another attraction is the Active Pass Lightstation at Georgina Point. Built in 1885 and replaced in 1940, the lighthouse and its grounds attract visitors who like to watch the ferries pass on their route through Active Pass.

Bays, coves, beaches, valleys and forested highlands offer plenty of opportunity for relaxation and recreation. At Mount Parke Regional Park a forty-five-minute hiking trail leads up to the two-hundred-and-seventy-metre-high peak. Families can picnic and play at Dinner Bay, or attend the annual salmon bake and join in on weekend celebrations such as Canada Day, B.C. Day and Labour Day.

Less accessible but equally impressive in its topography, vegetation and serenity is the Native Reserve at Helen Point located on the Active Pass side of Village Bay. Established in 1877 and still in the possession of members of the Cowichan band, the reserve was used as a fishing station for First Nations people more than four thousand and five hundred years ago.

About the Author

D. S. Hartley holds degrees in English Literature and Education, and has taught English as a Second Language for several years. She and her husband make their home wherever they are.

ISBN 142511637-X